My Heavenly Hockey Club

2

AI MORINAGA

Translated and adapted by Athena and Alethea Nibley
Lettered by North Market Street Graphics

DEL REY

BALLANTINE BOOKS • NEW YORK

My Heavenly Hockey Club volume 2 is a work of fiction. Names, characters, places, and incidents are the products of the author's imagination or are used fictitiously. Any resemblance to actual events, locales, or persons, living or dead, is entirely coincidental.

A Del Rey Trade Paperback Original

Published in the United States by Del Rey Books, an imprint of The Random House Publishing Group, a division of Random House, Inc., New York.

DEL REY is a registered trademark and the Del Rey colophon is a trademark of Random House, Inc.

Publication rights arranged through Kodansha Ltd.

First published in Japan in 2005 by Kodansha Ltd., Tokyo, as *Gokuraku Seishun Hockeybu.*

ISBN 978-0-345-49921-9

Printed in the United States of America

www.delreymanga.com

9 8 7 6 5 4 3

Translator/Adapter—Athena and Alethea Nibley
Lettering—North Market Street Graphics

Contents

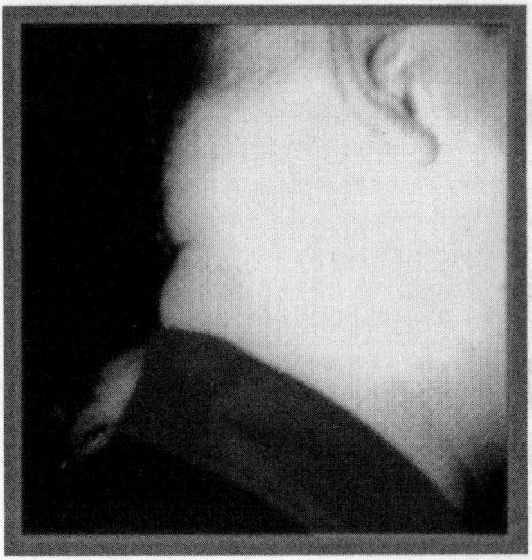

This is the bride and groom from my friend's wedding. Soon these two will be having their second child! When I found this, it took some time before I knew what it was a picture of.

Honorifics Explained

Throughout the Del Rey Manga books, you will find Japanese honorifics left intact in the translations. For those not familiar with how the Japanese use honorifics and, more important, how they differ from American honorifics, we present this brief overview.

Politeness has always been a critical facet of Japanese culture. Ever since the feudal era, when Japan was a highly stratified society, use of honorifics—which can be defined as polite speech that indicates relationship or status—has played an essential role in the Japanese language. When addressing someone in Japanese, an honorific usually takes the form of a suffix attached to one's name (example: "Asuna-san"), is used as a title at the end of one's name, or appears in place of the name itself (example: "Negi-sensei," or simply "Sensei!").

Honorifics can be expressions of respect or endearment. In the context of manga and anime, honorifics give insight into the nature of the relationship between characters. Many English translations leave out these important honorifics and therefore distort the feel of the original Japanese. Because Japanese honorifics contain nuances that English honorifics lack, it is our policy at Del Rey not to translate them. Here, instead, is a guide to some of the honorifics you may encounter in Del Rey Manga.

-san: This is the most common honorific and is equivalent to Mr., Miss, Ms., or Mrs. It is the all-purpose honorific and can be used in any situation where politeness is required.

-sama: This is one level higher than "-san" and is used to confer great respect.

-dono: This comes from the word "tono," which means "lord." It is an even higher level than "-sama" and confers utmost respect.

-kun: This suffix is used at the end of boys' names to express familiarity or endearment. It is also sometimes used by men among friends, or when addressing someone younger or of a lower station.

-chan: This is used to express endearment, mostly toward girls. It is also used for little boys, pets, and even among lovers. It gives a sense of childish cuteness.

Bozu: This is an informal way to refer to a boy, similar to the English terms "kid" and "squirt."

Sempai/Senpai: This title suggests that the addressee is one's senior in a group or organization. It is most often used in a school setting, where underclassmen refer to their upperclassmen as "sempai." It can also be used in the workplace, such as when a newer employee addresses an employee who has seniority in the company.

Kohai: This is the opposite of "sempai" and is used toward underclassmen in school or newcomers in the workplace. It connotes that the addressee is of a lower station.

Sensei: Literally meaning "one who has come before," this title is used for teachers, doctors, or masters of any profession or art.

-[blank]: This is usually forgotten in these lists, but it is perhaps the most significant difference between Japanese and English. The lack of honorific means that the speaker has permission to address the person in a very intimate way. Usually, only family, spouses, or very close friends have this kind of permission. Known as *yobisute,* it can be gratifying when someone who has earned the intimacy starts to call one by one's name without an honorific. But when that intimacy hasn't been earned, it can be very insulting.

My Heavenly Hockey Club

2

Ai Morinaga

Contents

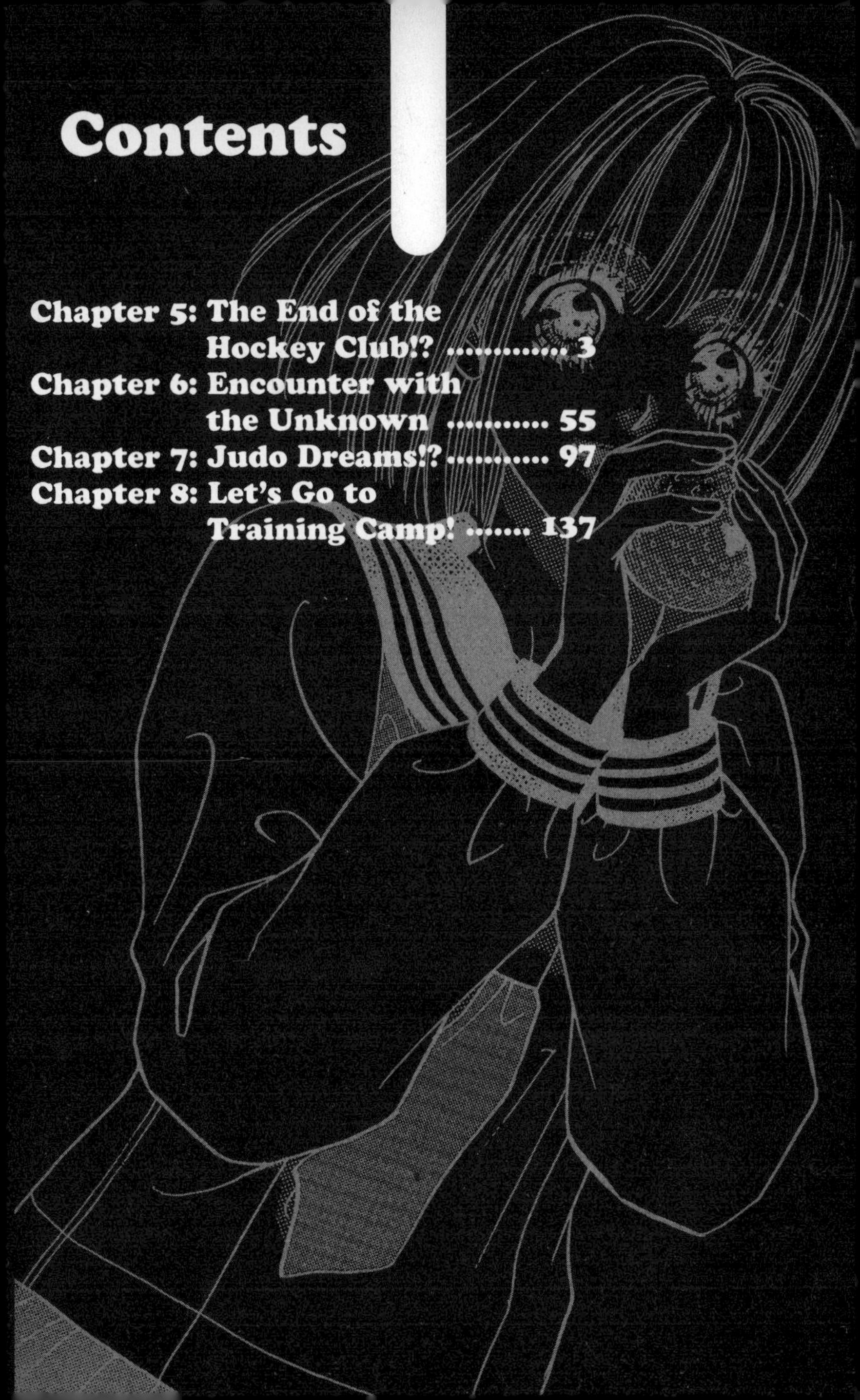

Chapter 5: The End of the Hockey Club!?

ZZZZ
ZZZ
ZZZ
SNORE
ZZZ... BURBLE
BURBLE
BURBLE
......
GRUMBLE

Quiet!
Hockey Club

Oof!?
WHUMP
My Heavenly

Field Hockey Club
Are you trying to kill me, Hana!?
Man!
Look at these abs. There's clearly a fist mark.
Eehh...
Well, it was loud and annoying.

I can't help it! I'm a living thing!
How dare you say that! *You're* the one who fell asleep on my stomach!
GATAAHH
Aahh, don't move, Izumi!
Don't say that! I was half asleep already!
GYAAAHH!
I didn't fall asleep on that hard stomach 'cause I wanted to.
It's the worst stomach pillow I've ever slept on!
...You sleep on people's stomachs that often?
It makes a lot of noise and it's un-comfortable to sleep on.
He was hungry. He is a growing boy, after all.
Here, I got some Kazan brand *Kamakura dorayaki*. Let's have tea.
PERK

But we ended up napping again today.
GOBBLE GOBBLE
ハフハフ
Because the weather's so nice this time of year.
GOBBLE GOBBLE
ハフハフ
We are the travel club, basically.
It's not like we have a match coming up, so why not?
Oh.
Now that you mention it,
isn't there a meeting for club presidents today?
I completely forgot.
That's right.
Wouldn't it be over by now?

はは Ha ha
Oh, well! We don't really need to go to budget meetings anyway!
はは Ha ha
Even if we did get a budget, it wouldn't even cover our snacks!
あは Ah ha
It's nice to use your own money.
They're mak-ing me sick...
ケッ Keh.
コンコン KNOCK KNOCK
Yes, coming, coming.
カチャッ KACHA
Ah!
ぽよん BOING
E-
Excuse me.
Pardon us.
May we have a moment?
ぱたぱた PAT PAT

Who's that again?
The new student body president and vice president, the Ota brothers.
We just had an election, remember?
Oh.
......
GLANCE
ちら
Akagiyama
What club are you?
Oh, sorry, sorry.
I was napping and forgot about the presidents' meeting.
...About what came out of that meeting.
Yeah.
We don't care how much we get for club expenses.
Do as you see fit.
Or whatever.
POP

You have one week to win a match, or the hockey club will be disbanded.
It was decided at the presidents' meeting.
Eh?

We'll let the tennis club have the vacant space.
We cannot afford to allow a club to occupy a room and grounds if they don't have sufficient activity.
We approved it without your consent, but it's your own fault you were absent.
Don't hold it against us.
One week?
You can tell us that...
SCRATCH SCRATCH
But no one will let us play with them since they all found out we had a bear as a goalie.
And we haven't practiced at all.
?
Word travels fast.
We've forgotten the rules.
A bear...?

Oh, it doesn't really matter. We can make a hockey field in my yard.
There's room at my place, too.
I'd like a bigger club room that we can use more freely.
Besides,
I'd like to have a match.
どん
DON
But when someone orders me to do something, I don't want to do it anymore!
フン
Hmph.

Izumi Oda.
You may be the chairman's grandson, but you won't get any special treatment from me.
I'm looking forward to the end of this week.
You.
山形
さくらんぼ
Y- yes!?
You've got some *anko* there.

Please, take one.
Th...
Thank you.
Man.
What's their problem? Coming in here while we're eating.
BATAN
The student body president's in the tennis club, isn't he?
Our tennis club is really good, and they've got a lot of members, so they don't have enough courts.
What's with that? He's just abusing his power.
The captain, right? And his brother's the manager.
It's cold. Make some more.
Ah ha ha. We don't want to hear that from Izumi, do we, Hana-chan?
Hey, Hana?
Hana-chan?

ぽー
BLUSH
Ha...
Hana-!!?

スパーン
THWACK
スパーンッ
THWACK
...Hmmmm

I saw something like this in a shojo manga a long time ago.
The picture of a maiden in love.
So *that's* her type.
Morons. She's more interested in food than the opposite sex.
As if.
Izumi.
But I've never seen Hana-chan like that.
Even Hana-chan is kind of a girl.
......
ばちっ
SNAP
ささっ
SASA

DOKI
DOKI
DOKI
DOKI
......
That's...
the girl from the hockey club, isn't it?
Can I help you?
START
Have you sched-uled a match?
Or did you come to complain?
N-no, not that.
I...

かあああーっ
BLUSH
Now, now.
Brother, she's a girl; you don't need to talk to her like that.
?
たーっ
TAH
E-
excuse me!
ドーン
WHAM
Kya!
Hana, let's go to the club.
Izumi-sempai.
Ow!

Hello!
Nice seeing you!
'lo!
What's wrong with it? Based on what they said yesterday, it seems like they'll let us have the hockey field.
I don't like it!!
I *will* crush that hockey club!
I hate their devil-may-care attitudes!
But I wonder if that girl likes you, Brother.

She couldn't look you in the face and kept looking down. It was so cute.
WHAT!!?
Oh, so that's why she was acting strange...
You sure are slow, Brother.
...I see.
She's not really my type, but that girl is correct.
Heh heh heh heh
Indeed. I am better than Oda, after all.
Did you see his face just now?
Likes flashy girls.
Arrogant as ever.
But it's almost refreshing to see such a modest girl these days.
Watching you from the shadows like that.
She's an endangered species.

Hey, Hana.
You've been act-ing weird since yes-terday.
Is some-thing bothering you?
Eh...?
You guys go on inside.
'Kay.
Take your time.
If there is some-thing, I'll listen, so tell me.
Eehh? Even if I told *you*, Izumi-sempai...

Gyaaahh!
Could it be Öta...?
Don't say it! You'll remind me!
That star-tled me...
Ha... Hana!?
....
Wh... when I look at him, I...
I'm over-come with emotion.
Wha!?
And I feel like I can't control myself. I...
I'm afraid, I guess...
Of, of what...!?
GULP

No. I just can't say it. It's too embarrassing.

This club room and the hockey field really do belong to the hockey club.
Eehh~~~?
We're having a match.
We *will* win, and protect it to the very end from the tennis club!!
TWITCH

The tennis club...!
B-BMP
B-BMP
どきどき
Takashi. I don't care if it's six-on-six or what, just find us a school we can play against.
Right, right.
Starting tomorrow, we have strict morning practice!
GATAN
Eh!?
No! You promised we wouldn't have any more morning practice!
Quiet. I've already decided.
TSUUUN
つーん
WHAT!?
Why do you think I worked so hard to get into a school I can walk to in three minutes!?
GATAAAN
We'll collect the entire cost of all the trips you've taken with us until now.
Now, now, Hana-chan. This time it won't even last a week. It'll be over in no time.
So cruel...!

The Nanbu Department Store is having a Hokkaido *bussanten* starting this weekend.
You like *bussanten*, don't you, Hana-chan?
When the match is over, let's go together. It'll be my treat.
We get the feeling anything that says Hokkaido on it has got to taste good.
I-in that case, then...
Then starting tomorrow, we meet at six a.m.!

I'm so stupid!!
It...
it *is* impossible...
They'll know I'm a girl for sure.
You're manly!!
ぼ
SHOONK
These guys...!!
In your case, Hana-chan, even without the padding, you'll be fine if you wear this!
In this area.
Izumi! Why don't you take a short break?
In a bit!

Hey, why did Izumi-sempai suddenly get so motivated?
Oh,
it's because...
ぼこん
WHACK
Ow!

Izumi, let's practice passing.
.....
?
Hana-chan, are you okay?
DOZE
DOZE
I'm fine...
I'm tired.
Bed...
Unngh, I just wanna sleep.
I'm only getting nine hours of sleep a day.
Looks like you've finally found an opponent.
GABAH
Why? At a time like this!
I hear you're thinking of having a match now?
Yeah.

Both teams are low on members, so it'll be six-on-six, though.
TWITCH
But a match is a match!
......
TWANG
GASP
N-n-n-no, I can't let him get near me now.
R-run away...!
AWAWAWA!
Well, all right. I won't go cheer you on, but good luck...
......
Good day.
SWOON

FLINCH
ビクッ
Hana—!?
What are you doing!?
A...are you all right?
Hang in there, Hana...
DOKI
DOKI
DOKI
DOKI
I'm fine, so don't come any closer.
ばたーん
BATAAAN
H-Hana!
Hana-chan!
ぐぉー
GUOOOOHH
......
Ah...
This feels good.

I'm finally in a bed.
I'm so happy...

Oh, you're awake.
You really need to fix that habit you have of falling asleep just anywhere.
We thought you were dead.
Th—
that scared me...
...Well, excuse me for being sleep-deprived.
Whose fault is it I have morning prac-tice...?
I'm taking you home, so you can get some sleep.
Y-yeah.
Drive.
Certainly.
......
VRRRROOM

...This is kind of uncomfortable.
Hey, Hana.
You...
Eh?
BRAKE
We're here.
30 seconds.
...It's nothing.
I'll come pick you up at one tomorrow.
Yeah.
Then good-night!
GARA
Hey, Hana.
Good luck.
For tomorrow's match.

Yay!
My bed
♡
♡
Hey!
Change
your
clothes!
......
ドドドドドドド
DODODODODODOH
All right,
everyone!

Today is our long-awaited first match, and our first victory!
We must win, at all costs
and protect our hockey club to the very end!!
Yeah!!
GAPO
Please don't let them find out...
B-BMP
B-BMP
B-BMP
B-BMP
Ah!
WINCE
MURMUR
It's a girl.
They have a girl on their team.
They found out!?
MURMUR

Why do they have a girl?
MURMUR ザワ
MURMUR ザワ
Is she the manager?
But she's cute... ♡
Even if she is flat...
?
にこ GRIN
にこ GRIN
Natsuki-sempai...
I lose...
Aw, man.
ぴく TWITCH
ぴく TWITCH
Please don't let any shots come my way.
Hey, Hana.

We're going to win.
Izumi-sempai...
PIIIIIIII
KAN
Izumi-sempai.
KAN
Oohh.
This is more of a match than I thought it would be.
I'm impressed with every-one.

Take this!
First shot!
GAH
Eh?

ガシャーーーンッ
GASHAAAAN

くど YADA
くど YADA
くど YADA
くど YADA
くど YADA
くど YADA
くど YADA
くど YADA
くど YADA
くど YADA
くど YADA
くど YADA
くど YADA
くど YADA
And?

He lectured us until dark and we couldn't finish the match.
......
Have some.
Tch.
And it looked like we could have had our first victory, too.
Then, as decided, the hockey club will be disbanded.
You will be giving us the hockey field and this room.
No.
We did kind of have a match, and it's not like we lost!
But you didn't win. Stop quibbling!
ふんぞーッ
HAUGHTY

Suzuki-san, was it?
Don't you hate it when a man doesn't know when to give up?
Eh?
W-well, yes.
We don't play much hockey anyway.
Isn't being the travel club good enough, Izumi-sempai?
DOKI DOKI
DOKI
And I'll never have to go to morning practice again. I would love that~~
Suzuki!
Hana-chan.
See? Your club member agrees with me.
...Hana, you
hate the hockey club that much...?
DOKIN
Oh yes, Suzuki-san.
Eh...?

When the hockey club is no more, would you like to join the tennis club?
Just a minute, Brother!
Not here!
You came to see us practice the other day, didn't you?
TWITCH
BLUSH
Th-that was...
BASH
Buh!
It's on!

You or me. Whoever Hana chooses wins!
Oh, man.
Then if you lose, the hockey club will disband?
Fine!
He trusts Hana-chan.
Why did he have to say that?
Hold on, Brother, calm down.
You, too, Oda-kun.
Both of you, cut it out...
Hana-chan?
Quiet!

Hana! Who's better? Him or me!?
I-
I...
can't...!

どかーんっ
CRASH
So, so comfy...
ハァ
HUFF
BOING
I knew it would be~~
ハァ
HUFF

Ah.
What's this, what's this, what's this~~?
Ah.
Aahh!
PAT
PAT
PAT
PAT
H–
Hey, Hana, stop that!
What is this flesh?
Hm?
Tell me.
Well?
What are you doing to my little brother!?
P-please forgive me~~
You can't do that!
Let go, Hana.
Let go!!
TUG
No~~~
TUG
I don't care if you arrest me; I'm going to sleep on this!
Sh-she won't come off...!!
TUG
She's asleep.
Ah.
Ungh-gh-gh...
ZZZZ
Help! Police!
Ah! Why you! Don't be so rough with her!
Hokkaido Bussanten
父の日のギフト

ジャガイモの花
But~~
I couldn't just ask him to let me touch him, so I was holding it in this whole time.
It's all good. Thanks to her, our club won't be disbanded.
It was an impressive draw due to injury.
Ah! This is good~~
Mixed feelings
Hey, Hana. Don't ever do anything like that again.
Aww. But he was such a good stomach pillow.
SLURP
Ah!
Izumi-sempai, can I have a *jaga*-butter?
Fine.
Yay ♡
One, please!
...If you want a stomach for a pillow, you can use mine.
No. Your stomach isn't comfortable to sleep on.
It's hard and noisy. It needs to be more, you know...

Local Delicacy Kokuma
Meso-Ramen
Tokachi
Azuki
amen
Azuki
NANBU
The hockey club was almost disbanded. But the crisis...
Suzuki-san! We're here to deliver your water-bed!
Eh!?
...has been averted, for now.
High-quality beds
Waterbed

The End

Chapter 6: Encounter with the Unknown

grypon
grypon
GRYPON

GOMA-FU

Oooh! Cherries!
Wow, they look good!
We've got tons of American cherries at home, so I'm sharing.
Help yourself.
Can I have some? Can I have some?
Let's eat!

ぽんっ
POP
ぱく
BITE
BITE
ぱく
And again.
Hana-chan, you can eat as many as you like.
Oh, well, it would be such a waste to eat it all at once.
What are you doing?
Sweeeet ♡
So

I'b newer eaden such dewicious chewwies in aww my wife~~
I'm glad you like them.
Eating all at once
YOINK BITE
YOINK BITE
DOHN
What are you saying?
If you're really Japanese, it has to be Sato Nishiki cherries!
Satô's time of death?
They're the smaller cherries with a brighter color.
Those are expensive, so my family could ***never*** have them.
Darn it.

Sato Nishiki cherries are expensive?
I don't know. Wouldn't they be? More expensive than American cherries, anyway.
Keh.
Making me sick as usual...!
CHALAAAN
Outl00k Express
...tasks completed
This screen will not display while sending
Errors
Receiving message(s)
......
Hey, Izumi.
Nn~~?
We've been challenged to a match.

That's great. This is a first.
No way! Where!?
Yamagata.
Yamagata...
?
It's decided, then.
Eeeehh!?

Our next away game, we'll go cherry picking!!
The local delicacy of Yamagata: Sato Nishiki
Eh? ♡
Yonezawa beef!
Yamabushi!!

Izumi, Hana-chan.
We're almost there.
VRRRRROOM
BRAKE
I'm sorry. I can't eat any more.
Ma'am, I'd like another all-Yonezawa-beef bento...
Come on, wake up!
Wow, this is a nice school.
Their club building is pretty, too.
Let's see, the hockey club's room should be...
カー部

Huh? We're at the end?
I wonder if we passed it.
......
Boys' Field Hockey Club. Now recruiting members.
山形の
おいしい
AUSTRALIA

Boys' Field Hockey Club. Now recruiting members.
...GULP
ごくり
.........?
山形の
おいしい
りんご

Electricity thief!!
START
SLAM
Is it the hockey club again!?
I keep telling you—don't use our electricity without asking!
Now, now. Don't be so stingy.
We can have a little.
There aren't enough outlets!
Captain, the electricity's been cut off~~
I guess we'll just have to get a long cord and use the baseball club's power.
DUMBFOUNDED
Ah.

Welcome!
Oohh!
Boys' Field Hockey Club. Now recruiting members.
Hockey clubs from the city really are different.
H—
hello...
Thank you for coming all this way.
Man, it's been a year since we've had a match. Everyone's all excited.

Our hearts are pounding, too...
Really?
It really is great to be able to play, ain't it?
BORON
FLINCH
Ah.
No problem, no problem.
Hey, get the duct tape.
Coming!
D-duct tape!?
You're gonna keep repairing it!?
We're a puny club that doesn't have enough members, so we don't get a club room or a budget.
We have to take care of the equipment we have.
And when you keep repairing it like this, you really feel attached to it.
2-C
Tanaka

I guess thrift and frugality are the basics of being Japanese, after all.
See? All done.
2-C Tanaka
That's wonderful...!!
We're impressed...!!!
Uh, is it really going to be okay...!?
R-really?
Clearly it would be better to buy a new one in this situation!
BASHFUL
PACHI
PACHI
PACHI
2-C Tanaka
What'll I do?
I have a bad feeling about this...
ta
Momotaro
Momo
ro
Momo

Card-board is pretty useful, huh?
Eh? Are you sure!?
Trade ♡
Th-then I'll draw a logo on it, free of charge ♡
SQUEAK
SQUEAK
Oooohhh, awesome!!
Hana!
Goodie!
What do you think, Hana!?
My heart grows heavy.
MEIRINKAN
Ehime
Aomori Apple
Potatoes

Trade...
Absolutely not!
Hey, that's enough. Let's practice. Practice!
Today was going to be our first victory for sure, wasn't it?
Ah!
くるっ
TURN
I'm leaving.
Hana?
Let's forget the match and go pick cherries.
スタ
STALK
スタ
STALK
What are you saying? *I'm* gonna play a match!
I just got brand-new shin guards!

But this thing's falling apart!
Even if we put duct tape on it, it'd fall down if someone passed gas!
And how would you fix a goal with duct tape anyway? It would definitely fall on me and kill me!
Your gloves are fixed with duct tape, aren't they?
Gloves are okay!
But please buy me some new ones.
Their captain was saying it would be fine.
Let's start the match!
Come on. Let's go, Hana.
I have to fix things with duct tape more often, so I know better than you, Izumi-sempai!!
2-B
Yamada

The owner says it's okay, so it's okay.
You have to take good care of things.
あ
Ah
Man, Hana, you're such a worrier.
はははは
Ha Ha Ha Ha
WHOOSH

GAH
MEIRINKAN
2
MEIRINKAN
10
I-I'm sorry. I'm so sorry!
I...
I'm fi...
SAG
Are you okay!?
DRIP
DRIP
DRIP
MEIRINKAN
Izumi!!
DRIP
DRIP
10

BATAAAAN
I *told* him...
......
Hana.
Let's go pick cherries.
Yay! Sato Nishiki!
Awww.
We didn't get to finish again.
Man.
STALK
STALK

Pl- please wait!
We'll fix the goal right away!
It's our first match in a year! Please don't go!
Don't bother! My life is more important than thrift and frugality!
Please! None of the places nearby will play against us!
I don't blame 'em!!
And we don't have the money to travel for away games.
If you have that kind of money, buy new sticks!!
Is that why you asked us?
I worked so hard to get into a school with a hockey club...
I'm sorry, everyone. I'm so worthless.
It's not your fault, Captain...!
...I kind of feel sorry for them.
Yeah.
Who cares! Hana and I were almost killed!
I wouldn't say *that*...

Um—
Whose side are you on, Hana!?
It's okay.
A club that's so blessed that they can afford to all travel for away games would never understand.
Of course not. There's no way I'd understand the feelings of a poor person!
MEIRINKAN

Waaaaahh!
わーっ
Hmph.
Wow, you're the worst!
How mean!
I'm not sure what that says about you as a person.
Izumi, even if you think those things, you shouldn't say them.
Yeah.
Excuse us for being poor!
Izumi-sempai, you...
Hurry up. You're picking cherries with us, aren't you?
Yay ♡
Sato Nishiki!
FILE
FILE
....
Uh...
Um...
If you're picking cherries, we can show you a good place not many people know about...

But please have a match with us.
All right, it's a deal!
In exchange, you will do as I say!
Eh...?
"As you say"...?
GACHA
ガチャッ
トゥルルル―
RRRRRING
Send me a complete set of hockey equipment right away.

Sorry to keep you waiting!
We have a delivery for an Oda-sama!
Cherry Shipping

Ah...!
Aahh!
Tanaka
My eyes...
I'm blind...!!

Like hell I'd risk my life just to play a match.
If you want to play with us, use these!
C...
can we?
With this, the nearby schools'll play you, too.
Be a man and throw away your old stuff.
STARE
GULP...
Re-ally...!?
Thank you...!
Izumi-sempai...
I'm looking forward to that place you mentioned.
2-A

Oh! It's been so long since I've smelled the aroma of new equipment!
Wow, Izumi-sempai.
This ball is the most expensive one in the catalog. ♡ ♡
You do come in handy sometimes.
Even though he was saying those things earlier...
Hey, hey, Izumi-sempai. What about my gloves?
Oh, I forgot.
Eeehh!?
Does it matter? They wouldn't really put anyone's life in danger.
Sigh. It really is nice unloading new equipment.
But it's too good to use!
You're right. Then for now, we'll carefully lock it away!

Well then.
STICK
STICK
Don't fix anything!!
2-C Tanaka
Weren't you listening to me!?
Why do you think I bought it!?
Now go get it, and line up!
B-but I get so scared when I think we might hurt the new equipment...
I don't care! Just hurry and get it out of its wrapping!!
Eehh!?
MEIRIN

I can't. I just can't. It's too dreadful...!
Me neither...!
Hey, guys.
Roger!
Ah!
Aahh, stop...!
RIP
RIP
NO!
Please, stop...!
RIIIP
RIP
RIP
RIP
RIP
There. Now you've given up, right?
We're play-ing a match. If we don't hurry, it'll get dark!
......

I-I'm so nervous I think I'm gonna pee myself...
Ah! I think I just did!
Ugh, poor people are so much work!
Let me see that.
?
Y-yes sir.
?
STALK
スタ
STALK
スタ
GONG

MARCH
MARCH
MEIRINKAN
10
There.
Now it's used; you can use it more easily.
Riz

BATAAAAN
バタ―ンッ
Captain!
1—B Azuma
2—B Yamada
Captain, hang in there!
JOOOOO
じょー
Aaahh!

Ugh, we didn't get to hear about the good place because Izumi-sempai did all that stuff.
Aww.
ちぇー
It's not my fault!
Poor people don't make any sense!!
Ooh, there's a lot here!
Well, it's compli-cated.
He said he couldn't use it if it's new; I was just helping out! Why did he faint!?
Izumi-sempai, these Sato Nishiki are really good!

BITE
ぱく
So
Sweeeet ♡
Nasuki-shempai, Hato Nihiki weawwy awe good ♡
GOBBLE
がふがふ
GOBBLE
I'm glad you like them.
You don't get sick of these as fast as American cherries.

What are you doing, Izumi-sempai?
You can eat as much as you want in the orchard, so don't waste time zoning out!
I can just buy some before I go home. Don't act so poor.
Buy some before you go home!?
Then what's the point in even coming to pick cherries!?
Using the price of admission into the orchard to eat even one more cherry before going home is the basics of picking!!
Don't act so spoiled!
Ouch!

Ugh, this is why I hate spoiled rich boys!
You don't get it!!
......
Hana-chan...
Come on, Izumi-sempai.
Don't just stand around; let's go.
KIRI
キリッ
Yeah!
He who eats most wins!
BITE
ぱく

So
Sweeeet ♡
The ones up top look yummier. There's lots left~~
No fair, Izumi-sempai!
Up here?
DROOOOOOL
NOD NOD
YOINK
BITE
YOINK
BITE
YOINK
BITE
Aaaaaaaugh!
Man, you're hopeless.
You are too immature!!
CLAP CLAP
Fine. I'll go get a stepladder!

Here.
YOINK
ひょい

ズル
SLIP
Ah!
GYAAAHH!
WHACK!
Augh!
THUD
On the way home, he bought me some Sato Nishiki for 500 yen a cherry.*
*$5
Izumi!!
Hana-chan, are you okay!?
But I was so nervous, I couldn't really taste them.
The End

Chapter 7: Judo Dreams!?

しと
DRIP
しと
DRIP
しと
しと
DROP

ウィーン
HUMMM
ウィーン
HUMMM
ウィーン
HUMMM
だら
LAZY
だら
LAZY
だら
LAZY
ピコ
BEEP
ピコ
BOP
あへ～
SIIIIIGH
ウィン
HUM
ウィン
HUM
ウィン
HUM

Aww, we're out of Shiomi manju.
GATAN
Should I get out the Furano milk pudding and double-fromage cheesecake?
PERK
Which would you like, Hana-chan?
Both ♡
BSSSSHHHHH
DROOL
Furano MILK

Yum...!
What is this!!?
Would you like some, Izumi?
Judo Dreams
When I'm done reading...
He's completely engrossed in it...
That manga is definitely addictive.
Like a little kid.
Mmm, Hokkaido food really is delicious!
I want some *uni*.
Some *nama-uni* from Rebunto.
Then maybe next time I'll order some *nama-uni*.
MUNCH
MUNCH

やったー!!
Yaaaay!!
Unidon ♡
Aaahh, that was good. ♡
ゲフー
PATAN
BELCH
It's all gone...
Awww.
むに
PINCH
BAH
Wha...
What are you doing?
Out of nowhere!

Hana, you've
gotten fatter.
SHOCK SHOCK
When I look down, there's fat in the way.
N...now that you mention it...
Because you sleep after eating.
Even seals get thinner when it gets warm out, normally.
MUKA

むにっ
PINCH
Look who's talking, Izumi-sempai.
Heh.
What is that about?
Aahh! My abs!
They're hiding!
...Now that you mention it,
maybe it's my imagination, but everyone looks rounder...
Well, we haven't practiced or anything, since it's been raining so much lately.
I have been thinking that the club room is more crowded recently.
I thought it was because of the massage chair, but I guess not.
......

Ah- ha ha ha ha
あはははは
At this rate, instead of the Hockey Club, we'll be the Chub Club!
Good one!
It's not funny!
...
Would you please stop it with the puns...!!
No more lying around just because it's the rainy season.
Starting today, we're doing honest club activities!
But we can't use the field.
Is there some exercise we can do inside?
Eh?
I've already decided on one.
I want to do the *Jigoku-guruma!*

Ji...?
"Jigoku-guruma" ...?
It's a certain kill move in the manga he was just reading.
Certain...!?
Judo, huh?
Why not?
Eh? J-just a!
Judo!?
Ooh, ooh, ooh! I wanna do it, too!
I'm in!
All right, it's settled! Starting today and for the time being, the Hockey Club will be the Judo Club!
Eeeeeehhh!?
Waaaahh!
PACHI!
PACHI
PACHI

Then, without delay...
Eh...?
Wh- what...?
Yah!
Someone get me a rubber band!
No! Stop!
Hey, hold her down there.
Come on, hold still. Stop strug- gling.
NOOOOOOO!
DRIP
しと
DRIP
しと
DROP
しと
DRIP
しと

Shaaaa!
Uraaaahh!
Doryah!
WHAM
The girls are intense as usual today.
Take that!
We'll have to work hard, too...
Whoa!

ガラン
RUMBLE
ズル
DRAG
ゴロン
CLATTER
ガコッ
BAP
ガコー
KAPOW
ズル
DRAAAAG
?
What's that noise...?
We are in your hands!
ゼゼ
ZEHH ZEHH

......?
Are you okay, Hana-chan?
W-would you quit going into things image-first already...?
Tying my hair up in a rubber band—this'll be a pain to get out. This is why I hate boys...!
Iron
TREMBLE
プル
TREMBLE
プル
TREMBLE
Wh-what's going on...?
Why is the Hockey Club...
wearing iron geta...?
ざわ
MURMUR
ざわ
MURMUR
......!
Which of you is the captain?
I-I am...
I guess...

The Hockey Club is going to be the Judo Club during the rainy season, so we'd like you to give us a place to practice.
Wha?
Uh, um.
I don't really understand...
We have a tournament coming up, and this is an important time for us to train, so I'm sorry, but...
Wh-why not, Kuruma-kun? We can give them a little corner.
Th-that's right. Don't be so stingy.
WHAM!
Please, go ahead.
Will this area do?
We're sorry it's so small.
Uh, um, just a...

Nn?
What?
No, nothing...
It's nothing...
Please excuse me...
We can't go against the girls!
All right.
If you ever need anything, please just ask.
Don't be shy!
SHOVE

Thank you.
あうん
SWOON

So the Field Hockey Club, now the Judo Club, will begin practice!
Yes, please!
Let's go, Hana!
POINT
Huh?
Deyaaah!
DAH
Eh!? Just a...

びょーーーん
WHOOSH
さっ
DUCK
どさっ
THUD
ずざーー
SKID
Why did you dodge!?
Of course I'm gonna dodge!!
What are you doing all of a sudden!?
It's no good, Izumi-sempai. For that move you need an opponent that's bigger than yourself.
Or you'll die.
What are they doing?
No clue...
Mm... I see.
All right, Takashi.
Yeah, yeah.
3cm
Whew.

Here I come!
GASHI
Yeah!
GAH
Ah!
That's...!

どべっ
DOBEH!
ふんぐぐぐ。。。
Nngh-gh-gh-gh...
しーーーん
SILENCE
......
Huh?
What's wrong? We're supposed to roll around on the ground here.
You won't even budge...
That's weird...
You're heavy.
It's really just impossible, don't you think...?

Oh yeah!
In the drama I saw on SkyPerfect, it was like this...
You take the ankles and bring them to the thigh...
I don't want to see you getting stuck in that position, so please stop.
Should I
be your partner?
Eh?
GAH!!
My body's bigger than yours, too, so I know it'll be okay!

Ah! No fair, Sempai!
Well I'm the only one bigger than Oda-kun, aren't I?
In terms of weight, I'm bigger, too!
I-I'm sorry.
I appreciate your sentiments, but...
We may be the Judo Club, but we can't use our moves on girls.
きゅうぅうん
TWAAAAAANG

What's that supposed to mean? You tried using a move on *me!*
Shh!
Quiet. I felt my life was in danger!
Oda-kun...!
WINCE
......
What's with that girl?
Why is there only one girl?
But that hair's in a rubber band, isn't it? That can't be a girl.
And Oda-kun tried a move on her, so wouldn't that mean she doesn't count as a girl?
That's not your bust, that's your chest measurement.
I win! B: 105cm*
SNIGGER
And she has no bust.
...Certain kill moves, huh...?

*41 inches

Come to think of it, I started judo because I wanted to try the *Jigoku-guruma*...
I read my dad's prized manga and loved it...
I saw it once on "100 Most Memorable Drama Scenes" and always wanted to try it.
That'd be great, doing a certain kill move...
Hey guys, don't be getting any weird ideas.
Come on, let's get practicing.
There's no time to play around.
We know. That's just in manga and on TV.
This year we're bringing back the *Kinshûki* for sure!
Yeah!
うーん
Hmmm
This is harder than I thought. Maybe we should look at the manga again for research.
だら LAZY
だら LAZY
だら LAZY
だら LAZY
This *tatami* feels good...
You're lowering our morale, so could I have you leave after all?

NGOOOHHH
Go! Candid photos!
Aahh!
Send me your pictures later!
They're sleeping, they're sleeping. ♡ ♡
Captain!
しと
DRIP
しと
DRIP
しと
DROP

BLOW
Mmm...
Who...?
Let's go, Hana!
Doryah!
Please stay away!
Gyaaahh!
GLANCE
ちらっ
まったくもう…
Ugh...
SNICKER
クス
SNICKER
クス
We win...!
WORN OUT
......

I'm tired...
I'm just gonna sleep. This is a pain...
Take that. ♡
POTEH
ぽ
Kyan ☆
That hurts. ☆ ☆
GLANCE
ちら
GLANCE
ちら
Uryah!
Hn!
Oohh! Izumi-sempai, just a little more!!
ZZZZ
すぴー
No good, huh...?
Tch.

Awww! One of my fake nails came off.
Are you okay? I have some glue.
......
It's...
it's kinda nice like this...
B-BMP
ドキ
Their charm...
B-BMP
ドキ
It's like there are girls here...
All right! One more time, Takashi!
Bring it on, Izumi!
Uryah!
Ah.

WHOOSH
Time out.
Who left this manga here? It's dangerous.
KA-THUD
I-Izumi!?
Hana-chan!
H-Hana!?
You okay!?
GABAH
GROPE
FLINCH
...GLAAAANCE

......
SNORE
I'm saved...!
What's wrong?
?
Oh, I thought I'd touched her breast again, but it was her stomach!
I was afraid that if she'd been awake I would have been killed for sure this time!
TWITCH
She's gotten fat so there's no difference anymore!
Iz-
Izumi...!
GAH

......!
Ha-Hana!
KICK!
Time out!
Wait...!
WAAAAHH!

どさっ
THUD
Th
......

That was awesome, Hana-chan!
He flew!!
Izumi!
Are you okay, Izumi!?
...Ha
Hana,
you...

Can do it! Just now!! That was a certain kill move!
GASHI!
POP
You did it! You're amazing, Hana!

You're the best!!
GOH
GYAAAAHH!

Wh-what are you doing?
H-Hana-chan, calm down!
Pervert!
Do it again! Do it again, Hana!
Whaaa!?
Hit me, Hana!
N-no, stay away from me!
Izumi-sempai, you pervert!!
WIPE
BSSSHHH
WIPE
RUB
RUB
WIPE
WIPE
BLACK

BOOM
Eep!
KIRI!
Oda-kun!

Let us have this girl!
Wha?
What's your name!?
Ha-Hana Suzuki...
That overhead throw was incredible.
We had almost forgotten what's really important...!
A woman really does have to be strong!
You can't do anything wearing fake nails!

Let's master the gentle way together!
Just a...!
Wait a minute!
No! I found her first!
Ah! Thief!
BAH
We're through being the Judo Club!
Ah! No, I said don't touch me, Izumi-sempai!
FILE
FILE
Aw, man, it's over already?

NOOOOOO!
どかーん
WHAAAAAM!
Out of the way!
They're getting away!!
うおおお
WHOOOOOOORAAA!
Don't let them escape! After them!
Stop!
They're even scarier than before...
I-Izumi-sempai, put me down!
No!
カラ
KARA
Let go of Suzuki-san!
No!
As the rainy season came to a close,
the Judo Club went back to being the Hockey Club.

The End

Chapter 8: Let's Go to Training Camp!

It's finally summer vacation. ♡
Yay! Yay!
Report Card
You seem happy.
Because starting tomorrow, I can sleep as much as I want!
Lucky. I have club activities every day.
Aw, man!
Sounds awful. Good luck. ♡
Well, I'm off!
I'll call you later!
Hey, Hana!

We're having a meeting.
Eh!? Just a...!
Lucky...
STALK
スタ
STALK
スタ
Summer vacation means training camp, of course!
Training camp!?

No! I'd decided I was going to sleep during summer vacation!
Have you decided where we're going?
Okinawa.
Because we just bought a summer home on a private island in Okinawa.
It doesn't have a hockey field, though!
But it does have a tennis court.
Okinawa, huh? We haven't been there in forever.
Recently, we've been going overseas for all our summer vacations.
Making me sick...!
What's with these people!?
We'll have to have some Ishigaki beef.
No, *sôki soba*.
I'd like to try a *goya* burger.
Blue Seal ice cream!
PERK
ぴくっ

I'll get a double chin again...
...No, no!
I finally got back to my normal weight!
It'll be nice to nap in a hammock.
Yeah.
...Ha
hammock...?
キ
KIIIIIIIIIIN

ZAZAZAZAZAH
It's been my dream to take a nap in a hammock. ♡
I see it.
Is that it?

わたたたたた
WATATATATA
I own it, so I go first!
Ah! No fair, Izumi-sempai!!
We have another; I'll set it up.
Children...
至福
Bliss
I love Okinawa.
I'm glad I pushed myself to wake up early to come here.

ぽつ
DRIP
Rain...?
I fell asleep...
Aahh!?
Ham...!!
No way! Six o'clock already!?
Where is every-one...?
We had the manager take us out on a boat to the next island so we could ride the water buffalo. You wouldn't wake up no matter how hard we tried, so we went without you. We'll be back by this evening.
Lunch is in the refrigerator, so please eat it when you've woken up. We'll buy some Ishigaki beef for dinner.

……
Ugh, there's no helping it.
I'm starving.
Won't they be getting back soon?
You won't have any room for the Ishigaki beef.
Goya, beni-imo, and sugarcane.
Give me all of them!
There's pineapple and Blue Seal ice cream, too.
HOOOOWWWL

...The typhoon has changed its course to northwest!
It's gaining strength and speed...
...Natsuki-sempai and the others sure are taking a long time.
I wonder if they're okay.
RRRRR
Hello?
Ah, Izumi?
Takashi!

Where are you!?
HOOOOOOOOWWWWL
We're still on the next island.
We were all shopping and it got late.
What!? I can't hear y—
Sorry; we can't make it back today.
It got here sooner than I expected.
I'll bring the car around.
Eh? What?
Can you hear me?
ZAAAAHH
I think we can make it back by tomorrow morning...
CLICK
TSUUU
TSUUU
I got cut off...
Will those two be okay?
......
They'll be fine. It's Izumi-sempai and Hana-chan, after all.
Although it would be more fun if something did happen.
あははは
Ah ha ha ha

Izumi-sempai? What did he say?
......
TSUUU
TSUUU
...They can't make it back today...
Eh...?
Eeehh? Then what about dinner!?
You're still hungry?
Well I was looking forward to the Ishigaki beef.
Awww.
Have it cooked for morning steak or something tomorrow.
Then I won't save any of this, and eat it all.

Continuing the report on the typhoon
It's gaining force and approaching the Okinawa area...
9 pm
3 pm
Large scale typhoon approaching Okinawa. Strong wind warning.
BEEP
It's all stuff about the typhoon.
I wonder if anyone's showing anything else.
Yeah.
Right here!
Can you all see it?
There is clearly something resembling a pale human hand!
The true identity of the white hand that appears in the darkness!

真剣
Serious
This is not a good spirit.
ゴクリ...
GULP...
It is the spirit of a woman who committed suicide in this area.
It seems she died leaving a lot of resentment.
ガタ
RATTLE
Something strange appeared in the photograph our staff took here.
ガタ
RATTLE

BACHI
WAAAHH!
Ah.
A black-out.
It's pitch black...Izumi-sempai, where are the flashlights?
Uh, yeah, I think they were around here...
That startled me...
Here's one!
PAT PAT
ぽんぽん
Hey, Hana, I found one!
KACHI

GYAAAAAHHH!
Taking advantage of the confusion! Where do you think you're touching!?
KAPOW
Augh!
I-it was beyond my control! I thought I was patting your back!
COUGH
Well, I'm sorry that there's no difference between my back and my front.

じっとり
GLARE
Th-the lights aren't coming back, so let's just go to bed!
Man, that Hana.
How's she gonna make it up to me if my face scars?
Oww...
Now I'm all sweaty.
Guess I'll take a shower...
ZAAAAHH
Let's see...
Rax
Super R
shampoo
じ
STARE
Shampoo...
...is it this one?

RATTLE
ガタ
RATTLE
ガタ
......
...I was watching that TV show
Uh-oh...
so I feel like there's something behind me...
ビクッ
START
ガターン
GATAN
RATTLE
ガタ
RATTLE
ガタ
ガタ
RATTLE

DROP
PAH
Ah,
the lights.
Oh good, they're back on.
KACHI
DA
DA
DA
Whew.
SLAM
DA
DA
Eh?

WHAM

Ha!
WHAAAAAMMM!
GYAAAAAHHH!
H-Hana! Open up!
Izumi-sempai!?
Ow ow ow ow...
PUSH
PUSH
Fatty
Wh-wh-wh-what is with you all of a sudden!?
Please, open the door!
Never mind, just hurry!
No!
No!
SQUIIIIIIIISH
Fatty

GACHA
PEH
SLAM!
Th-
that scared me...
Ugh, what is with him?
BADUMP
...Come to think of it,
we're here alone tonight, aren't we...?
He showed me himself naked before. Is he an exhibitionist?
BADUMP
BADUMP
It can't be that Izumi-sempai...
It can't be.
That's stupid; I'm going to sleep.
Fatty

...But he did grope me earlier.
......
I don't think so, but for now...
Just in case.
Fatty
STAGGER...
...Dammit!
You remember this, Hana!
I thought she was gonna kill me...!
PEEEEER
BACHI
BACHI
BACHI
BEEP

This should do it!
BRIGHT
We've had as much rain in an hour as we have all season...
I'm sorry, Denko-chan...
Please don't go near the coastline...
BRIGHT
Now, let's go to sleep!
That thing in the bathroom was my imagination.
SNUGGLE
It's because it was after watching that thing on TV. Unlike Hana, I'm delicate!
It still hurts...
...Still, that Hana. She didn't have to squeeze me in the door like that...
HUH

Ah.
Again...
......
It's okay. Be strong!
If I just go to sleep, it'll be morning before I know it!
RATTLE
ガタ
RATTLE
ガタ
RATTLE
ガタ
...Was it really
my imagination...?

さきっ
SKITTER
がばっ
GABAH
......

ペ
PETAH
たー
SKITTER
!
Something's
here...
WHOOSH
BASH

Hanaaaaa!
DA-DA-DA-DAH
DODAH
START
Hey, Hana, open up!
POUND
POUND
POUND
Izumi-sempai...!
POUND
Hurry!
Open up! Open up!
POUND
POUND
No...

No!
GACHA
GACHA
GACHA
POUND
Shut up! I'm telling you to open the door!
POUND
No way.
It can't be. Is Izumi-sempai really...!?
POUND
GACHA
No!
Stay away!

WHOOOOOOOOOOSH
CRASH
I-if I run away, I'll die for sure...!!
CRASH
AWAWAWAWAH
Th-the palm trees are at a 90-degree angle...!!
SLAM

HAA HAA
HAA HAA
But earlier he said he couldn't tell the difference between my back and my front.
Izumi-sempai, you'd take anyone who's female!?

Hana...!
どきん
DOKIN
Eh...?
Th-

There's a ghost on my back...!!
Gh?
A-a ghost dropped on me from the ceiling...!
WAAAHH! It moved!
モゴ
MOGO
Just...
just a minute.
GOSO
GOSO
....

Is this the ghost?
Eh?
......
TWITCH
TWITCH

Huh. It says there are lots of geckos in Okinawa.
It says they're guardian deities of homes, so please don't treat them roughly.
Mm-hm
Mm-hm
Now let it go.
There.
What the heck...
BLUSH
Izumi-sempai is so misleading...
Bururu: Okinawa
Beach vacations, starting with what to do at your hotel.
'05
......
It wasn't a ghost.
Well good for you.
...pff
D-
Don't laugh! It's your fault for changing the channel!

WHAT!?
If you didn't like it, you could have changed the channel yourself!
Shut up!
GYAAH!
GYAAH!
What are we going to do about this?
Everyone will be shocked when they get back.
Doesn't matter. It's my house.
I'm sorry. You can use any of the free rooms.
I'm tired, so I'm going to sleep.
SMIRK
SMIRK
The lights aren't back on yet; will you be okay without me?
Are you okay by yourself now?
....
Fatty

I'm not okay.
Eh?
どきん
DOKIN
...I meant to be sarcastic...

Up to here is my territory.
If you cross this line, you will be mercilessly punished.
I know already!
Oh well...
Then goodnight.
Dangerous weapon
'Night.
....

POKE
ちょん
SHOONK
GYAAAAHH!
Y-you don't have to do it so hard!!
Shut up! Go to sleep!!!

SNORE
...Did something really happen...?
But *what*...?
It can't be...

See you in volume 3 ♪

The End

Superdeluxe Four-Frame Comic, number 1

My Heavenly Chub Club 1

When they were just lying around during the rainy season,
they got fat.
Fast-forward
Indeed.
We need to lose weight.

Superdeluxe Four-Frame Comic, number 2

My Heavenly Chub Club 2

SNOOOOORE
Economy size
When she slept right after eating during the rainy season,
she got fat.
FAT
TURN
No fair!
It's not fair!
You can tell us it's not fair, but...
It's more disturbing to look at us than you.

Superdeluxe Four-Frame Comic, number 3

On the way to the convenience store, I passed by a young man whose chest was jiggling violently on the uneven pavement.

It was a bitter-sweet feeling, so I tried drawing it.

Is it true that when you get fat it starts with the chest?
A little hopeful...
ぺたり
FLAT
......
Diet, diet!
ゆっさ
JIGGLE
ゆっさ
JIGGLE
Ah!?
What are you doing, Hana?
Stop...!
SIGH
もみ
GROPE
もみ
GROPE
もみ
GROPE
もみ
GROPE
ああっ

The End ♡

Ai Morinaga-sensei Speaks! ~Kind of a Good Story~

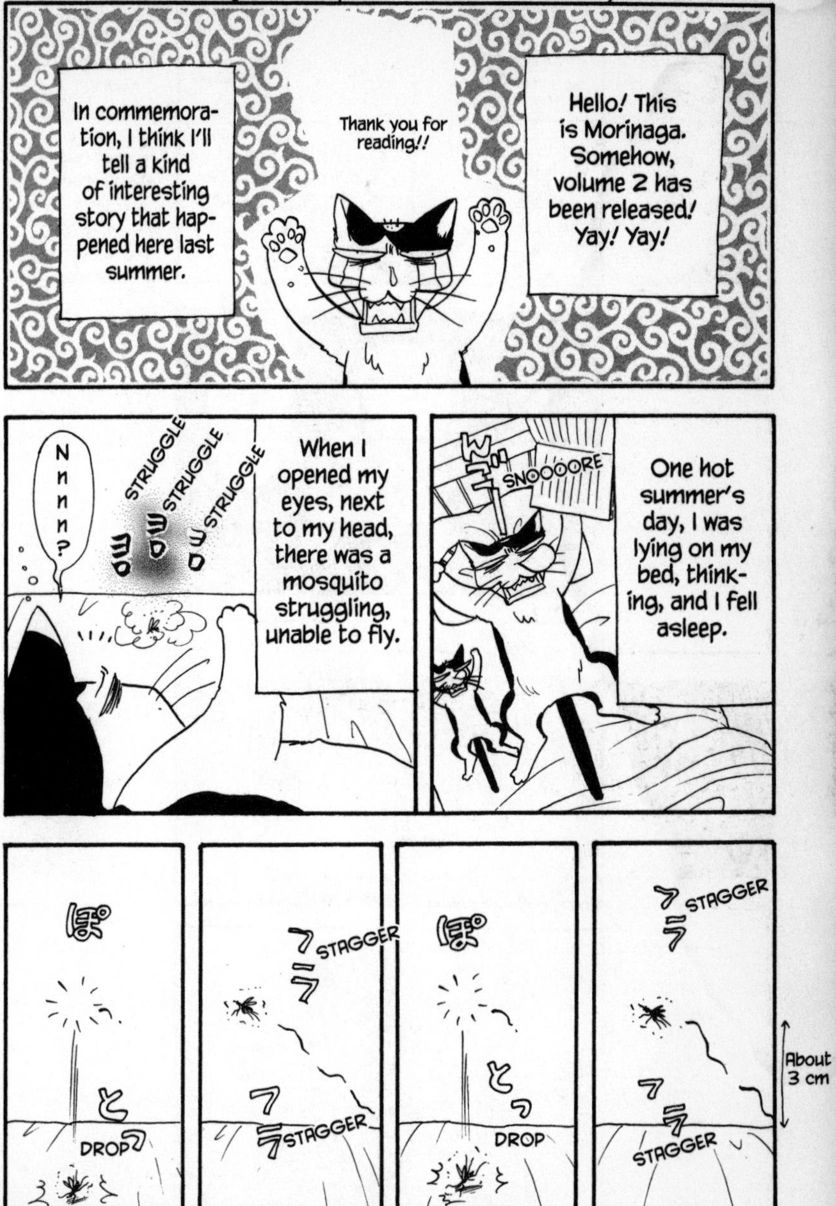
Hello! This is Morinaga. Somehow, volume 2 has been released! Yay! Yay!
Thank you for reading!!
In commemoration, I think I'll tell a kind of interesting story that happened here last summer.
One hot summer's day, I was lying on my bed, thinking, and I fell asleep.
SNOOOORE
When I opened my eyes, next to my head, there was a mosquito struggling, unable to fly.
STRUGGLE
STRUGGLE
STRUGGLE
Nnnn?
STAGGER
STAGGER
About 3 cm
DROP
STAGGER
STAGGER
DROP

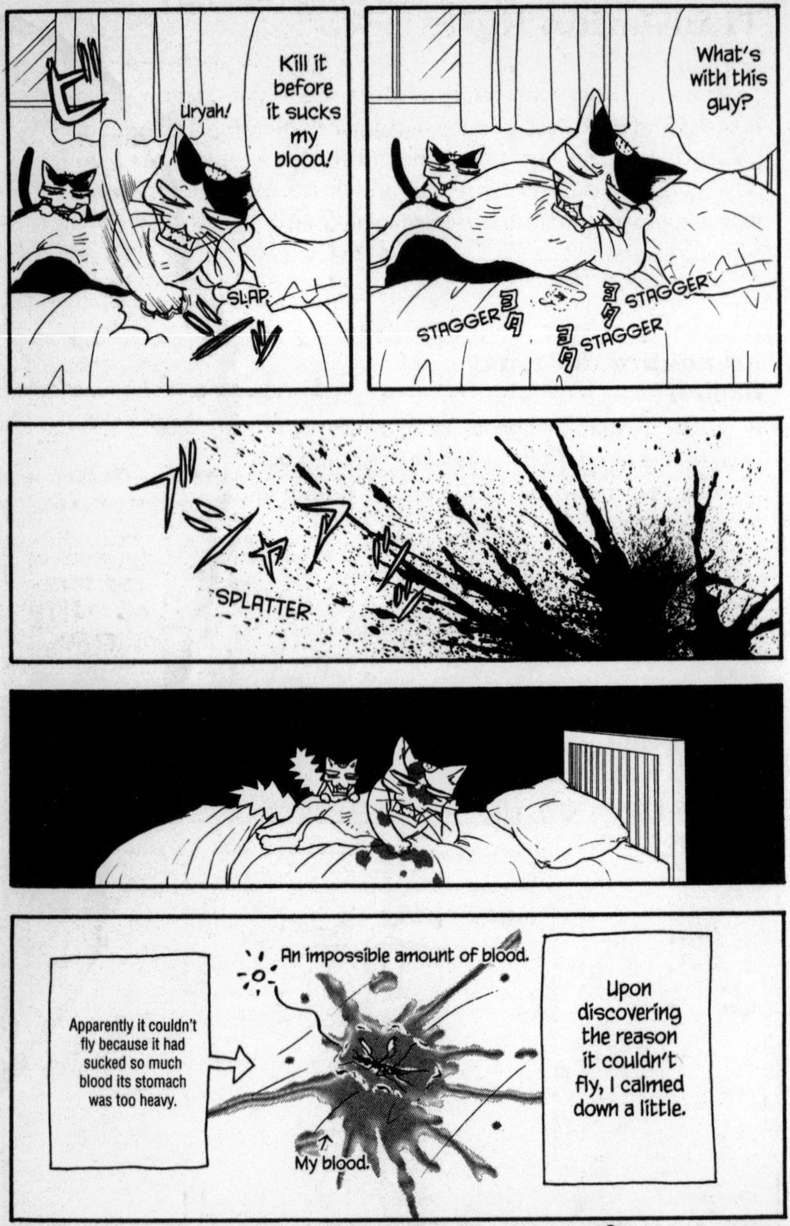
What's with this guy?
STAGGER
STAGGER
STAGGER
Kill it before it sucks my blood!
Uryah!
SLAP
SPLATTER
Upon discovering the reason it couldn't fly, I calmed down a little.
An impossible amount of blood.
My blood.
Apparently it couldn't fly because it had sucked so much blood its stomach was too heavy.

Now please look forward to volume 3

Translation Notes

Japanese is a tricky language for most Westerners, and translation is often more art than science. For your edification and reading pleasure, here are notes on some of the places where we could have gone in a different direction in our translation of the work, or where a Japanese cultural reference is used.

Kamakura dorayaki, page 8

A Japanese snack made of bean paste sandwiched between flour pancakes. Apparently it is the favorite food of the popular Japanese animated character Doraemon.

He was hungry. He is a growing boy, after all.
Here, I got some Kazan brand *Kamakura dorayaki*. Let's have tea.
PERK

Akagiyama, page 11

Akagiyama is a volcano in central Japan. The pennant's significance is that it's a souvenir, and not related to hockey as much as it is to traveling.

You've got some *anko* there.

Anko, page 15

Anko is a red bean paste.

Bussanten, page 29

Bussanten literally means "goods shop." A department store will hold a kind of fair at which they sell foods from different regions of Japan. In this case, Hokkaido, the northernmost island of Japan, is being showcased.

The Nanbu Department Store is having a Hokkaido *bussanten* starting this weekend.
You like *bussanten*, don't you, Hana-chan?
When the match is over, let's go together. It'll be my treat.

***Jaga*-butter, page 52**

A baked potato with butter.

Hey, Hana. Don't ever do anything like that again.
Aww. But he was such a good stomach pillow.
SLURP
Izumi-sempai, can I have a *jaga*-butter?

Local Delicacy
Meso-Ramen
Tokachi Azuki
amen
Azuki
NANBU

***Azuki* and *meso-ramen*, page 53**

Azuki means "red beans." *Meso* is a type of small eel, so *meso-ramen* is noodles served with eel.

Sato Nishiki and Satô's time of death, page 59

Sato Nishiki is the name of a famous kind of Japanese cherry grown mainly in Yamagata prefecture. But since Hana hasn't heard of it, she makes up her own interpretation of the term. Satô is a common Japanese name, and *shiki* can mean "time of death."

If you're really Japanese, it has to be Sato Nishiki cherries!
Satô's time of death?

Eh?
♡
Yonezawa beef!
Yamabushi!!

Yonezawa beef, page 62

Yonezawa is found in the Yamagata prefecture, and its beef is considered to be among the best beef in Japan.

Yamabushi, page 62

Yamabushi were originally warrior monks and ascetics—monks who dedicate themselves to their religion by abstaining from all worldly desires. Today, *yamabushi* refers to modern ascetics. In Yamagata, there is a place where people can experience *yamabushi* training, which includes fasting, meditating under waterfalls, and walking on fire.

Momotaro, page 69

Momotaro is a character from Japanese folklore, and the name is used here as a brand name. Momotaro was born from a peach, so it seems appropriate that a produce company would take his name.

ta
Momotaro
Momo

Should I get out the Furano milk pudding and double-fromage cheesecake?
Aww, we're out of Shiomi manju.
PERK

Shiomi manju, page 99

Salty cakes.

Furano milk pudding and double-fromage cheesecake, page 99

Both are foods they most likely got at the Hokkaido *bussanten*. Apparently the best milk pudding in Japan is made in Furano, a city in Hokkaido.

Judo Dreams, page 100

Judo Dreams, or *Judo Icchokusen (The Straight Line of Judo)*, is a manga about a boy who wants to be the world judo champion that was made into a popular TV drama in the 60s and 70s.

When I'm done reading...
Judo Dreams

Mmm, Hokkaido food really is delicious.
I want some uni.
Some nama-uni from Rebunto.
Then maybe next time I'll order some nama-uni.
MUNCH
MUNCH

Uni, _nama-uni_, and Rebunto, page 100

Uni is sea urchin, and *nama-uni* is raw sea urchin. Rebunto is an island in Hokkaido.

Unidon, page 101

Don is a large bowl, so *unidon* would be an *uni* served in a large bowl.

やったー!!
Yaaaay!!
Unidon ♡
Aaahh, that was good. ♡
ゲフー
PATAN
BELCH

あははは
Ah ha ha ha ha
At this rate, instead of the Hockey Club, we'll be the Chub Club!
Good one!
It's not funny!
...

Chub Club, page 104

Since *bu* means "club," and *debu* means "chubby" or "fat," they are considering being the "*de-bu*" instead of the *hockeybu*.

Jigoku-guruma, page 104

Jigoku-guruma means "Hell Wheel" and is the certain kill move made famous by *Judo Dreams*.

I want to do the Jigoku-guruma!

Are you okay, Hana-chan?
W-would you quit going into things image-first already...?
Tying my hair up in a rubber band—this'll be a pain to get out. This is why I hate boys...!
Iron
TREMBLE
TREMBLE
TREMBLE

Iron _geta_, page 109

Geta is the kind of footwear the Hockey Club is now wearing. Iron *geta* are worn by characters in manga such as *Judo Dreams* to help the martial artists get stronger.

SkyPerfect, page 117

A TV network in Japan.

In the drama I saw on SkyPerfect, it was like this...
You take the ankles and bring them to the thigh...
I don't want to see you getting stuck in that position, so please stop.

This year we're bringing back the *Kinshûki* for sure!
Yeah!
This is harder than I thought. Maybe we should look at the manga again for research.

Kinshûki, page 120

The *Kinshûki*, or Golden Eagle Flag, is the prize for the national high school judo tournament held each year in Japan.

Tatami, page 120

A straw floor covering used for Japanese-style rooms. Because judo is a Japanese art, they would use a Japanese room to practice in.

LAZY
LAZY
LAZY
LAZY
This *tatami* feels good...
You're lowering our morale, so could I have you leave after all?

Let's master the gentle way together!
Just a...!

The gentle way, page 135

Another name for judo.

Ishigaki beef, *sôki soba*, *goya* burgers, and Blue Seal ice cream, page 140

We'll have to have some Ishigaki beef.
I'd like to try a *goya* burger.
No, *sôki soba*.
Blue Seal ice cream!
ERK

Ishigaki beef is high-quality beef from the Okinawa area. *Sôki soba* is a dish of noodles with a big piece of pork on top. *Goya* is a vegetable in the gourd family, grown in Okinawa. Blue Seal is a brand of ice cream, like Baskin-Robbins.

Goya, beni-imo, and sugarcane.
Give me all of them!
There's pineapple and Blue Seal ice cream, too.

Goya, *beni-imo*, and sugarcane, page 145

These are all flavors of Blue Seal ice cream. *Beni-imo* is a red-purple sweet potato.

Denko-chan, page 160

This should do it!
BRIGHT
I'm sorry, Denko-chan...
Please don't go near the coastline...
BRIGHT
We've had as much rain in an hour as we have all season...
Now, let's go to sleep!

Denko is the name Izumi made up for the electricity that he is using in so much excess. *Denki* means "electricity," and many Japanese girls' names end in *-ko*.

Preview of Volume 3

We're pleased to present you a preview from volume 3. Please check our website (www.delreymanga.com) to see when this volume will be available.

You need to be getting to the banquet hall to entertain our guests soon.
Yes, sir.
Well, thanks to Hana's dinner, I do feel like I'm up to doing this.
Shall we be off!?
Yeah!!
I'm glad...
I'll be out to help you later.
Try your best.
Leave it to us.

Have some more, miss.
Your glass is empty.
Have you had too much to drink?
Your face is red...
I think I might be drunk, too.

I'm hot...
ぐい
TUG
ごくり
GULP

Over here.
I have low body heat. Shall I cool you off?
Oh, you're right. You feel nice and cold.
It's true that fat stays cool.
Maybe I'll take my clothes off, too.
BAH
What's wrong with us? I feel kind of weird.
I feel so hot...

M-me, too!
RUMBLE
KYAAAAAAHH
I have low body heat, too!!
They're trying *too* hard...
Wh-
what on earth is going on...?

Hey, let go!
Takashi-kun, where are you!?
Why you little girls! I'm first!
Natsuki-kuuuun!
G... grand-ma...
GYAAAH
GYAAAH
Where are the twins!?
PARA
Nn?
PARA
TWITCH
Huh? Izumi-kun!?
Izumi-kun, where did you go?
Oh, Hana.
What'll I do?
Am I sick or something?
DRAG
DRAG
Wh-why!?
Stay away from me!

SHIKI TSUKAI

MANGA BY TORU ZEKU
ART BY YUNA TAKANAGI

DEFENDING THE NATURAL ORDER OF THE UNIVERSE!

The *shiki tsukai* are "Keepers of the Seasons"—magical warriors pledged to defend the planet's natural order against those who would threaten it.

When 14-year-old Akira Kizuki joins the *shiki tsukai,* he knows that it'll be a difficult life. But with his new friends and mentors, he's up to the challenge!

TORU ZEKU
YUNA TAKANAGI
1
SHIKI TSUKAI

Special extras in each volume! Read them all!

VISIT WWW.DELREYMANGA.COM TO:
- Read sample pages
- View release date calendars for upcoming volumes
- Sign up for Del Rey's free manga e-newsletter
- Find out the latest about new Del Rey Manga series

RATING T AGES 13+

DEL REY MANGA デルレイ
The Otaku's Choice™

KITCHEN PRINCESS

STORY BY MIYUKI KOBAYASHI
MANGA BY NATSUMI ANDO
CREATOR OF ZODIAC P.I.

HUNGRY HEART

KITCHEN PRINCESS
1
custard pudding
taramasalata
rainbow colored jelly
christmas cookie
onion gratin soup
Story by MIYUKI KOBAYASHI
Manga by NATSUMI ANDO
Creator of Zodiac P.I.

Najika is a great cook and likes to make meals for the people she loves. But something is missing from her life. When she was a child, she met a boy who touched her heart—and now Najika is determined to find him. The only clue she has is a silver spoon that leads her to the prestigious Seika Academy.

Attending Seika will be a challenge. Every kid at the school has a special talent, and the girls in Najika's class think she doesn't deserve to be there. But Sora and Daichi, two popular brothers who barely speak to each other, recognize Najika's cooking for what it is—magical. Could one of the boys be Najika's mysterious prince?

Special extras in each volume! Read them all!

VISIT WWW.DELREYMANGA.COM TO:
- Read sample pages
- View release date calendars for upcoming volumes
- Sign up for Del Rey's free manga e-newsletter
- Find out the latest about new Del Rey Manga series

RATING T AGES 13+

DEL REY MANGA デルレイ
The Otaku's Choice

Mamotte! LOLLiPOP

MICHIYO KIKUTA

BOY CRAZY

Junior high schooler Nina is ready to fall in love. She's looking for a boy who's cute and sweet—and strong enough to support her when the chips are down. But what happens when Nina's dream comes true . . . twice? One day, two cute boys literally fall from the sky. They're both wizards who've come to the Human World to take the Magic Exam. The boys' success on this test depends on protecting Nina from evil, so now Nina has a pair of cute magical boys chasing her everywhere! One of these wizards just might be the boy of her dreams . . . but which one?

Michiyo Kikuta
1
Mamotte!
LOLLiPOP

Special extras in each volume! Read them all!

VISIT WWW.DELREYMANGA.COM TO:

- Read sample pages
- View release date calendars for upcoming volumes
- Sign up for Del Rey's free manga e-newsletter
- Find out the latest about new Del Rey Manga series

RATING T AGES 13+

DEL REY MANGA デルレイ

The Otaku's Choice

Sugar Sugar Rune

BY MOYOCO ANNO

QUEEN OF HEARTS

Chocolat and Vanilla are young witch princesses from a magical land. They've come to Earth to compete in a contest—whichever girl captures the most hearts will become queen! While living in a boarding school, they must make as many boys fall in love with them as possible if they want to achieve their goal. Standing against them are a pair of rival princes looking to capture their hearts because they want to be king!

There's danger for the witch-girls, though: If they give their hearts to a human, they may never return to the Magical World....

Sugar Sugar Rune
1
Moyoco Anno

Ages: 10+

Special extras in each volume! Read them all!

DEL REY

VISIT WWW.DELREYMANGA.COM TO:
- View release date calendars for upcoming volumes
- Sign up for Del Rey's free manga e-newsletter
- Find out the latest about new Del Rey Manga series

TOMARE!

止まれ

[STOP!]

You're going the wrong way!

Manga is a [illegible]pletely different type of [illegible] experience.

To start at the beginning, go to the end!

That's right! Authentic manga is read the traditional Japanese way—from right to left. Exactly the opposite of how American books are read. It's easy to follow: Just go to the other end of the book, and read each page—and each panel—from right side to left side, starting at the top right. Now you're experiencing manga as it was meant to be!